FROGS

by Meg Gaertner

Cody Koala

An Imprint of Pop!

popbooksonline.com

abdobooks.com
Published by Pop!, a division of ABDO, PO Box 398166, Minneapolis, Minnesota 55439. Copyright © 2019 by POP, LLC. International copyrights reserved in all countries. No part of this book may be reproduced in any form without written permission from the publisher. Pop!™ is a trademark and logo of POP, LLC.

Printed in the United States of America, North Mankato, Minnesota

092018
012019

 THIS BOOK CONTAINS
RECYCLED MATERIALS

Cover Photo: Shutterstock Images
Interior Photos: Shutterstock Images, 1, 5 (top), 5 (bottom left), 5 (bottom right), 7, 8–9, 10, 14 (bottom), 19, 20; A. Cosmos Blank/Science Source, 13; Christina Rollo/Alamy, 14 (top); Gary Meszaros/Science Source, 17

Editor: Charly Haley
Series Designer: Laura Mitchell

Library of Congress Control Number: 2018950115
Publisher's Cataloging-in-Publication Data
Names: Gaertner, Meg, author.
Title: Frogs / by Meg Gaertner.
Description: Minneapolis, Minnesota: Pop!, 2019 | Series: Pond animals | Includes online resources and index.
Identifiers: ISBN 9781532162084 (lib. bdg.) | ISBN 9781641855792 (pbk) | ISBN 9781532163142 (ebook)
Subjects: LCSH: Frogs--Juvenile literature. | Amphibians--Juvenile literature. | Pond animals--Juvenile literature. | Amphibians--Behavior--Juvenile literature.
Classification: DDC 597.81--dc23

Hello! My name is

Cody Koala

Pop open this book and you'll find QR codes like this one, loaded with information, so you can learn even more!

Scan this code* and others like it while you read, or visit the website below to make this book pop.

popbooksonline.com/frogs

*Scanning QR codes requires a web-enabled smart device with a QR code reader app and a camera.

Table of Contents

Amphibian

Frogs are **amphibians**. They can live on land and in water. There are more than 4,000 types of frogs. Most live in warm, wet areas.

Watch a video here!

Frog Facts

Frogs cannot turn their heads to look around. They have large eyes to help them see. Special eyelids protect their eyes underwater.

Learn more here!

Frogs have **webbed** feet
for swimming. They have
strong back legs for jumping.

Most frogs have smooth skin. Frogs must keep their skin wet.

Many frogs use their coloring to hide in their surroundings. Others use bright colors to surprise their **predators**.

A frog can die if its skin dries out.

Chapter 3

Frog Food

Frogs use their sticky tongues to catch food. They can move their tongues faster than a person can blink.

Learn more here!

Frogs eat insects and small animals. They cannot chew their food. They swallow it whole.

When a frog swallows, its eyes sink down into its head. The eyes help push the food down the frog's throat.

Frogs do not drink water. They take it in through their skin.

Chapter 4

The Life of a Frog

Female frogs lay eggs in fresh water. The eggs hatch in a few days or weeks. **Tadpoles** come out.

Complete an activity here!

Tadpoles live underwater. Over time, they grow legs. They grow **lungs** for breathing air. They lose their tails. They grow into adult frogs in a few months or a few years.

Making Connections

Text-to-Self

Have you ever seen a frog? If not, have you seen another animal in the wild?

Text-to-Text

Have you read another book about a different animal? How is that animal similar to a frog? How is it different?

Text-to-World

Frogs can live in water and on land. What other animals can do this?

Glossary

amphibian – an animal that lives fully underwater when it is young and then grows to be able to live on land.

female – a person or animal of the sex that can have babies or lay eggs.

lung – the part of an animal used for breathing air.

predator – an animal that hunts other animals for food.

tadpole – young frog or toad.

webbed – connected by a thick piece of skin.

Index

Online Resources

popbooksonline.com

Thanks for reading this Cody Koala book!

Scan this code* and others like it in this book, or visit the website below to make this book pop!

JAN 2020

popbooksonline.com/frogs

*Scanning QR codes requires a web-enabled smart device with a QR code reader app and a camera.